A Gentoo mother penguin with her two babies.

Those Perky Penguins

Sarah Cussen

Illustrations by Steve Weaver

Pineapple Press, Inc.
Sarasota, Florida

Copyright © 2011 by Sarah Cussen
Manufactured in October 2011

All rights reserved. No part of this book may be reproduced in any form or by any means, electronic or mechanical, including photocopying, recording, or by any information storage and retrieval system, without permission in writing from the publisher.

Inquiries should be addressed to:

Pineapple Press, Inc.
P.O. Box 3889
Sarasota, Florida 34230

www.pineapplepress.com

Photo Credits

Cover ©Rechitan Sorin/Dreamstime.com; Pages 2 and 32 © Leksele/Dreamstime.com; Pages 8 and 20 © Gentoomultimedia/Dreamstime.com; Pages 10 and 44 © Ekaterina Pokrovsky/Dreamstime.com; Pages 5, 14, 16, 22, 32 (baby), 40, 42, 46 © Guillaume Dargaud; Page 18 © Andrey Armyagov/Dreamstime.com; Page 24 © Vulnificans/Dreamstime.com; Page 26 © anky10/Dreamstime.com; Page 28 © Kitchner Bain/Dreamstime.com; Page 30 © Jan Martin Will/Dreamstime.com, inset © Jordan Tan/Dreamstime.com; Page 34 © Betsy Hern/Dreamstime.com; Page 36 © Vladimir Seliverstov; Page 49 photos of Garison Medlin by Jan Lee Wicker; Page 50 June Cussen; Page 52 satellite © Adastraperaspera/Dreamstime.com, crab © Michael Elliott/Dreamstime.com; Page 53 squid © Wksp/Dreamstime.com, tuxedo © Crazy80frog/Dreamstime.com.

Library of Congress Cataloging-in-Publication Data
Cussen, Sarah, 1980-
Those perky penguins / Sarah Cussen ; illustrations by Steve Weaver. -- 1st ed.
p. cm.
Includes index.
ISBN 978-1-56164-504-6 (hb : alk. paper) -- ISBN 978-1-56164-505-3 (pb : alk. paper)
1. Penguins--Juvenile literature. I. Weaver, Steve, ill. II. Title.
QL696.S473C87 2011
598.47--dc23
2011016099

First Edition
10 9 8 7 6 5 4 3 2 1

Printed in China

To Mark

An Adelie penguin considers jumping in.

Contents

1. Can penguins fly?   9

2. Are penguins birds?   11

3. How many kinds of penguins are there?   13

4. Why do penguins wear tuxedos?   15

5. Do penguins get cold?   17

6. What do penguins eat?   19

7. What do penguins drink?   21

8. Are penguins scared of polar bears?   23

9. Do penguins have knees?   25

10. How much time do penguins spend swimming?   27

11. How long can penguins hold their breath?   29

12. How big are penguins?   31

13. What are penguin feathers like?   33

14. Where do penguins lay their eggs?   35

15. What do baby penguins look like?   37

16. Where in the world do penguins live?   39

17. Do penguins migrate?   41

18. Why do some mother penguins leave their eggs?   43

19. Do penguins sing?   45

20. What are the dangers to penguins?   47

Activities

    Science project: How warm is blubber?   48
    Make a yummy penguin   50

Where to learn more about penguins   51

Glossary   52

About the author   54

Index   55

A Macaroni penguin takes a leap.

Can penguins fly?

No. Their wings are very small, and instead of helping them fly, their wings act as flippers to help them swim. Have you ever seen a penguin under water? They look like they are flying!

A Magellanic penguin

Are penguins birds?

Yes! They may not be able to fly, but they are still birds. Penguins, like all other birds, have feathers, wings, two legs, lay eggs, and are warm-blooded. They also live in large groups like many other birds. Penguin groups, called colonies or rookeries, can have thousands of birds.

How many kinds of penguins are there?

When you think of a penguin, you probably picture the Emperor penguin, which is what you often see in movies or at the zoo. But there are 17 species, or types, of penguins. (Some scientists say there are 18 types. They divide the Rockhoppers into northern and southern.) All penguins have dark feathers on their backs and light bellies.

Are these Emperor penguins discussing who has the nicest tuxedo?

Why do penguins wear tuxedos?

Penguins may look like they are dressed up for a party, but their dark backs and light stomachs are actually very practical. Their coloring helps protect them from predators. Other animals, like seals, sea lions, and killer whales, hunt and eat penguins. Penguins' dark backs make them hard to see from above. Their white bellies are the same color as the ice or sky above them, so they are hard to see by animals hunting from below.

Not enough blubber?
Wear a coat!

Do penguins get cold?

Just like any warm-blooded animal (like you!), penguins need to keep their bodies warm. Their outer feathers are waterproof, so they can dive in the freezing water. The feathers closest to their bodies are down, just like a warm comforter. Also they have an extra layer of fat, called blubber. Some kinds of penguins huddle close together to keep warm in the winter. Galapagos penguins live near the equator and have to be careful not to get too hot.

These two penguins have raced to the bottom for these bits of food.

What do penguins eat?

There is a reason penguins are so fast under water, even though they look awkward on land. All their food is under water. Penguins have to swim fast to catch fish, squid, and small crustaceans (sea animals with a shell, like shrimp, crabs, or krill). Penguins catch their slippery food with their bills. They hold onto it with their spiny tongues. Then they swallow it whole while swimming.

A Macaroni penguin takes a drink.

What do penguins drink?

People know better than to drink sea water, no matter how hot and thirsty they might be. But penguins can drink salty sea water because their bodies remove the salt from the water. They get rid of the salt through their noses. Penguins can also drink fresh water when they are on land.

This little Adelie penguin is trying to look scary to defend her nest.

Are penguins scared of polar bears?

If they met, a penguin might be scared of a polar bear! But lucky for penguins, polar bears live in the Arctic, very far north. Penguins live only in the Southern Hemisphere, or the southern half of the Earth. Some penguins do have to defend their nests from other animals who might eat their eggs.

This Gentoo penguin shows off his waddle.

Do penguins have knees?

When you pretend to walk like a penguin, you probably waddle around without bending your knees. But actually, penguins do have knees. You just can't see them, because they are covered by their feathers. They waddle because they have short legs. But just because they have knees, doesn't mean they have elbows!

Humboldt penguins are shy and swim alone.

How much time do penguins spend swimming?

Penguins love to swim. They can move much faster in the water than they can on land. And it's in the water where they find their food. Some types of penguins spend more of their time in the water than they do on land. They might go to sea for months, coming to shore only to lay eggs.

Magellenic penguins live in Argentina, Southern Chile, and the Falkland Islands.

How long can penguins hold their breath?

Most penguins dive under water for less than a minute. Lucky for them, their favorite fish are not very far down. But Emperor penguins like to eat larger fish and squid that live deeper. The longest dive ever timed is 21 minutes! Usually Emperor penguins stay under water around two to eight minutes.

Little Blue penguins

A big Emperor penguin meets a little Adelie. They both live in Antarctica.

How big are penguins?

The Emperor penguin is the largest type of penguin. An adult is about three feet seven inches tall and can weigh more than 75 pounds. That is the same height as a five-year-old human, and even heavier! The smallest penguin is the Little Blue penguin. It grows to 16 inches tall and weighs about two pounds, about the same as the average pineapple. The Little Blue is also called The Fairy penguin.

This adult Emperor penguin is molting.

This young Emperor penguin is losing his baby feathers

What are penguin feathers like?

To stay warm and dry, penguins have a lot of short, wide feathers—about 100 feathers per square inch. Every bit of their skin is covered with these hard little feathers. The feathers keep the penguin's skin nice and dry during their cold dives in the water. Every year they molt, which means they lose their old feathers and grow new ones.

Two Gentoo moms, one with an egg,
the other with a baby trying to hide.

Where do penguins lay their eggs?

Like all birds, penguins lay eggs. They need a good place to keep the eggs safe until they hatch. Gentoo and Adelie penguins make piles of stones to keep their eggs from rolling away. Emperor and King penguins don't build nests. They tuck their eggs on their feet under their bodies to keep them warm. Little Blue (or Fairy) penguins dig little holes called burrows.

Emperor penguins live a long time. This baby might live to age 50.

What do baby penguins look like?

Baby penguins are called chicks. After they hatch from their shells, most penguin chicks are covered in fluffy down. They look like little cotton balls. The down can be white, gray, black, or brown, depending on the type of penguin. This fluffy coat isn't waterproof, so the chicks must stay out of the water and wait for their parents to feed them fish.

Where in the world do penguins live?

Emperor

King

Adelie

Rockhopper

Chinstrap

Galapagos

Little Blue

Penguins live on the islands and coasts of the Southern Hemisphere. They live in Antarctica and in the most southern parts of Australia, New Zealand, Africa, and South America. Some of the places they live are a little bit warmer than you might think. But they always live near cool water.

39

Do penguins migrate?

Most types of penguins migrate, or move from one place to another and back again. Like other birds, they do this to feed or to find a good place to have their young. Some penguins do not go far, but some go thousands of miles. We don't know much about penguin migration. Scientists try to track them by using satellites. It's not easy since they are in very cold places and under water much of the time.

Two Emperor dads check an egg while they wait for the moms to return.

Why do some mother penguins leave their eggs?

Most penguin parents take turns keeping their egg warm, so the other parent can go fishing. But Emperor penguins are different. The mother travels a long way to go fishing while the father keeps the egg warm. He stands still in the cold for two months with no food, holding his egg on his feet. He keeps it safe until it is ready to hatch. Then mother returns with fish for the baby.

Megellanic penguins can bray, moo, and cackle.

Do penguins sing?

It depends on what you think singing is! Penguins don't sing like the songbirds in your yard. They have a loud call, more like a squawk than a song. They call to find their mates, to say hello, and to warn off other penguins or animals coming too close.

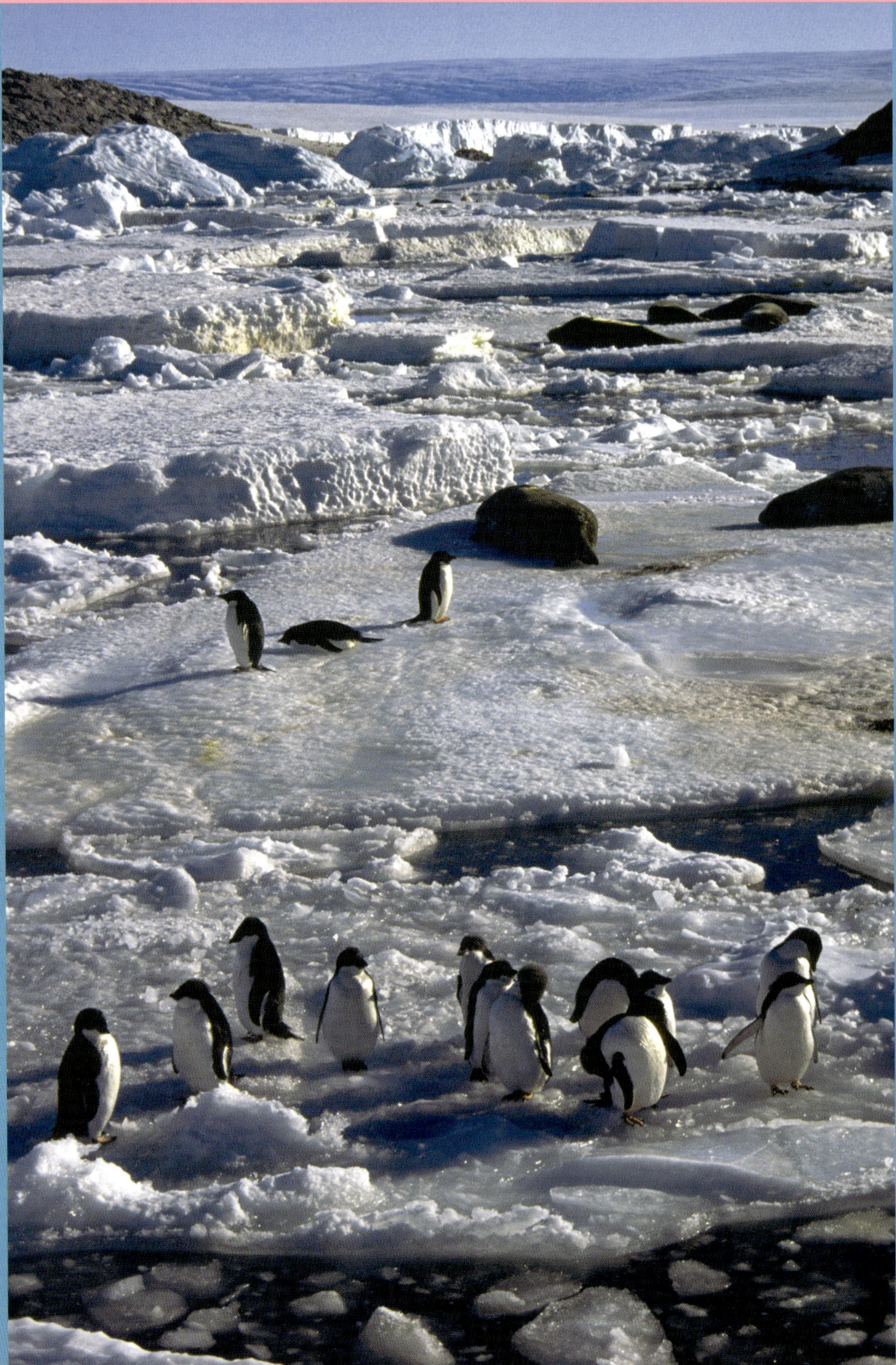

What are the dangers to penguins?

Humans have made life harder for penguins. We have caught too many of the fish penguins like to eat. We are putting too much pollution, especially oil spills, into the ocean waters. We think the ocean is so big it won't matter, but it does. And the climate is getting warmer. This means there is less ice for penguins to live on. We need to learn all we can about penguins so we know how to protect them.

Activities

Science project: **How warm is blubber?**
You learned that one of the reasons penguins stay warm in such cold weather is because they have an extra layer of fat (blubber). Now you can see how it works.

What you need
- bucket of ice water
- plastic bags
- shortening (such as Crisco)
- tape

What to do
First, half fill a plastic bag with the shortening. Shortening is a type of fat usually used in baking. Leave enough room for your hand in the bag.

Then, cover your hands with plastic bags and have someone help you tape them so they stay on. Be sure to tape only the plastic, not your skin. Use tape you can easily break when you want to take the bags off.

Put one hand covered in a plastic bag inside the bag of shortening. Tape that bag around your hand too.

Test the water with your hand without shortening. Feel how cold it is!

Then test the water with the hand in shortening. Does it feel warmer? Let your classmates feel the difference in your two hands.

Make a yummy penguin

What you need

    two Oreo cookies

    one candy orange fruit slice

    a black licorice stick (if possible)

    a dinner knife

What to do

Open one Oreo cookie and make sure the white filling is on one side. Break the other side in half and place it on top as shown for the wings. Open the other cookie and use it for the head.

Cut some little ends off your licorice stick for eyes. This makes cute "wheel eyes." But if you don't have licorice, you can just use a bit of cookie.

Cut three triangles from the orange candy slice, one for the beak, the other two for the feet.

After you show it off, you can eat your penguin!

Where to learn more about penguins

Books

Akesson, Susanne, and Brutus Ostling. *Penguins*. Harper, 2007.

Schreiber, Anne. *National Geographic Readers: Penguins*. National Geographic Children's Books, 2009.

Simon, Seymour. *Penguins (Smithsonian)*. Collins, 2007.

Websites

National Geographic Kids
http://kids.nationalgeographic.com/kids/animals/creaturefeature/emperor-penguin/

Seaworld Animal Infobooks
http://www.seaworld.org/animal-info/info-books/index.htm

Film

The March of the Penguins. Directed by Luc Jacquet. 2005.

Glossary

Blubber: A thick layer of fat underneath the skin of sea animals like penguins or whales.

Burrow: A hole or tunnel dug by a small animal.

Crustacean: Animals mostly living in the sea that have a hard outside shell (such as lobsters, shrimp, or crabs).

Down: Soft and fluffy feathers.

Flipper: The broad and flat limb sea animals use for swimming.

Galapagos: A group of islands in the Pacific Ocean 600 miles off the coast of South America. These islands have unique animals.

Hemisphere: Half of the earth, either divided North to South or East to West.

Huddle: To crowd or gather closely together.

Krill: A type of small crustacean (*see Crustacean above*).

Migration: Moving from one place to another at the same time every year. Animals might migrate for better weather for feeding, for example.

Molt: To shed or lose hair, feathers, shell, or skin, so a new coat can take its place.

Predator: An animal that lives by killing and eating other animals.

Rookery: The place where a group of birds or animals builds their nests and raises their babies.

Satellite: A machine in the sky circling the Earth.

Squid: A sea animal with eight arms and two longer tentacles, a long thin body with a fin on each side, and an internal shell.

Species: A category of living things of the same kind.

Tuxedo: A suit for men worn on special occasions.

Warm-blooded: Able to keep up a warm body temperature, even if it is cold.

About the author

Sarah Cussen also wrote, for this series, *Those Peculiar Pelicans*, *Those Terrific Turtles*, and *Those Beautiful Butterflies*. When she isn't busy learning about penguins, turtles, butterflies, and pelicans, she works for a charity that works on building peace in the world. She currently lives in London.

Index

*(Numbers in **bold** refer to photographs.)*

Adelie penguin, **5**, **12**, **22**, **30**, 35, 39
Africa, 39
African penguin, **12**
Antarctica, 30, 39
Argentina, 28
Australia, 39
Baby penguins, **32**, **34**, **36**, 37, 43
Birds, 11, 35, 41, 45, 52
Blubber, 16, 17, 48, 52
Chile, 28
Chinstrap penguin, **12**, 39
Colonies, 11
Crustaceans, 19, 52
Eggs, 11, 23, 27, **34**, 35, **42**, 43
Emperor penguin, **12**, 13, **14**, 29, **30**, 31, **32**, 35, **36**, 39, **42**, 43
Erect-crested penguin, **12**
Fairy penguin, *see* Little Blue penguin
Falkland Islands, 28
Feathers, 11, 13, 17, 25, **32**, 33, 52
Fiordland penguin, **12**
Fish, 19, 29, 37, 43, 47
Galapagos penguin, **12**, 17, 39

Gentoo penguin, **12**, **2**, **24**, **34**, 35
Humboldt penguin, **12**, **26**
Killer whales, 15
King penguin, **12**, 35, 39
Krill, 19, 53
Little Blue penguin, **12**, **30**, 31, 35, 39
Lobster, 53
Macaroni penguin, **12**, **8**, **20**
Magellanic penguin, **10**, **12**, **28**, **44**
Nests, **22**, 23, 35, 52
New Zealand, 39
Polar bears, 23
Predators, 15, 53
Rockhopper penguin, **12**, 13, 39
Rookeries, 11, 53
Royal penguin, **12**
Seals, 15
Sea lions, 15
Shrimp, 53
Snares Island penguin, **12**
South America, 39, 52
Squid, 19, 29, 53
Yellow-eyed penguin, **12**
Warm-blooded, 11, 17, 53

Here are the other books in this series. For a complete catalog, visit our website at www.pineapplepress.com.

Each title in the Those Amazing Animals series, written for children ages 6–9, has 20 questions and answers, 20 photos, and 20 funny illustrations by Steve Weaver.

Those Amazing Alligators by Kathy Feeney. Discover the differences between alligators and crocodiles. Learn what alligators eat, how they communicate, and much more.

Those Beautiful Butterflies by Sarah Cussen. Learn all about butterflies—their behavior, why they look the way they do, how they communicate, and why they love bright flowers.

Those Big Bears by Jan Lee Wicker. Why do bears stand on two legs? How do they use their claws? How many kinds are there? What do they do all winter?

Those Colossal Cats by Marta Magellan. Meet lions, tigers, leopards, and the other big cats. Do they purr? How fast can they run? Which is biggest?

Those Delightful Dolphins by Jan Lee Wicker. Learn the difference between a dolphin and a porpoise. How do dolphins breathe? What do they eat? Just how smart are they?

Those Excellent Eagles by Jan Lee Wicker. Learn all about those excellent eagles—what they eat, how fast they fly, why the American bald eagle is our nation's national bird.

Those Funny Flamingos by Jan Lee Wicker. Why are these funny birds pink? Why do they stand on one leg and eat upside down? Where do they live?

Those Lively Lizards by Marta Magellan. Meet lizards that can run on water, some with funny-looking eyes, some that change color, and some that look like little dinosaurs.

Those Magical Manatees by Jan Lee Wicker. Why are they magical? How big are they? What do they eat? Why are they endangered and what can you do to help?

Those Outrageous Owls by Laura Wyatt. Learn what owls eat, how they hunt, and why they look the way they do. How do they fly so quietly? Why do horned owls have horns?

Those Peculiar Pelicans by Sarah Cussen. Find out how much food those peculiar pelicans can fit in their beaks, how they stay cool, and whether they really steal fish from fishermen.

Those Terrific Turtles by Sarah Cussen. You'll learn the difference between a turtle and a tortoise, and find out why they have shells. Meet baby turtles and some very, very old ones.

Those Voracious Vultures by Marta Magellan. Learn all about vultures—the gross things they do, what they eat, whether a turkey vulture gobbles, and more.